I 'Like' Who I Am...
I 'Love' Being Me!

Written by: Patrice Lee

Illustrated by: Francesco Paolo Ardizzone

"I Like Who I Am ...I Love Being Me!"
Copyright, 2017
43 pages

Leep4Joy Books, a Division of Feinstein and Associates
Printed in the United States of America

All rights reserved. No part of this book may be reproduced or transmitted in any form or by any means without written permission from the author.

Library of Congress Catalog-in-Publication Data
ISBN: # 978-0-9863167-6-0

Edited by: Cathryn Williams
Consultation, Special Edits: Chelynne Lee, Stephen Moore
Illustrator: Francesco Paolo Ardizzone
Page Layout/Graphic Art: Bob Ivory, Jr., IvoryCoast Media

Please send all correspondence to:

Feinstein Development and Associates, P.O. Box 48172, Oak Park, MI 48237 or PatriceALee@gmail.com

Dedicated to children everywhere, because we want you to **"...live life happy!"** It's what the animals do -- every day.

My Animal Friends

This book is about animals and the funny things they do. Each one is very different. They have personalities too.

They come in many different patterns, prints, furs, solids and stripes. It doesn't matter that they're different. They love livin' life.

The great thing about them is they find comfort in their own space. Yet, they are lovable and adaptable in someone else's place.

Some are loud, and some are quiet. Some are big, and some are small. With so many beautiful ones to choose from, you just want to love them all.

If an animal is your pet, there's a lot of love to give. It doesn't matter how old you are, or where in the world you live.

Some are comforting. Some are cozy. Some are wet and sloppy too. On a day that you aren't feeling well, they'll be there just for you.

How can you live without them? Some say it's easily done. But, if you're like most of us, you're going to connect with at least one.

So take your pick of animal types, be it large or small. There's quite a selection of them -- striped, speckled, short and tall.

Hairy or hairless, curly or straight, there's an animal pet for you. Even if you've never had one you'll still know what to do; because most pets come with instructions. So, just follow the rules.

Stop! Look! . . .and Take Note!
{This cute little story happened to me}

As I left the post office today I saw this adorable family - a mommy and a daddy, and three baby geese. And when they approached the curb, all traffic ceased.

As our light turned green, you should've seen how they walked and wobbled as they crossed the street without fear. The mommy and the daddy kept in sync with babies staying near.

All of the geese walking tall, as each passenger and driver sat spellbound, looking on in awe. Oh, what a sight it was to look at! What a sight it was to see! The babies determined to keep up with Mom and Dad, altogether three. How lovely it was to see them strut, and for them to do it with such ease!

Traffic was stopped in every direction, while drivers, who waited patiently, never even beeped. For all eyes were fixed upon this family as they crossed the busy street.

We gave them our full attention as they wobbled, as they walked. Oh, to know what they were thinking ...if only they could've talked!

It's as if the geese were saying, if they could have spoken. ". . . Welcome to my world!" . . .as each one of us took note.

Animal Kingdom "Love"

Animals are confident and secure.
The cold and the heat they endure.
The sun, snow or rain; they trek through it all.
They don't complain.

They're not worried about bullies.
Nor concerned with how they look.
They're consistently careless and clueless;
And fancy-free with the foot.

They live free of pride and prejudice; free of jealousy.
Animal pets look for love from you and me.

Now surely there are some animals we can do without.
But, those are not the animals that I'm talkin' about.

So I'll start my introduction. And as I share with you,
Take a look at the animals from a different perspective,
And a new point of view.

What better way to begin than with an ant or a bee,
For these two little insects you'll certainly see
On any bright and beautiful, hot, sunny day,
As you work outdoors, or while you play;
Or, if you simply happen to get in their way.

So we'll start with the "***ant***," and take a look at the "***bee***."
We've got a whole book to read together, just you and me.

The "*Ant*" and the "*Bee*"
*How small are "**we?**"*

Ant: "Hey! I'm the busy little ant, and she's the worker bee. I do all of my work on the ground. She makes honey in a honeycomb, way up in the trees.

I'm always building and constructing. I make good use of your debris. While the bee is busy making honey for all humanity."

"So unlike the bee, I run away from people, I flee humanity."
Bee: "Because of who I am, people run away from me." ;)

Ant: "Now there are many other animals, who don't look at all like me. You can find them in the ocean, in the forest, in the trees; In the sky, and on the ground. You'll have to see it to believe!"

Ant: "But, I'm just an itty, bitty little **Ant**; and she's the sweet little, honey **Bee.** I like who I am, and I love being me."
Bee: "And I like who I am, and I love being me. The two of us together call ourselves "**we**." *(we-e-e-e)*

. . .Yes, I like who I am!
I love being me!
I'm the itty bitty **Ant**.
And she's the little worker **Bee**.

"Go to the ant, …consider her ways, and be wise. …she prepares her bread in summer and gathers her food in harvest" (Proverbs 6:6,8ESV).

I'm as light as a feather. I fly fancy and free.
My thin skin has many colors. There are many varieties of me.
My visit makes you happy. You smile when I go by.
Who am I? I'm the beautiful "**butterfly.**"
{You can find me on the page with the ant and the bee.}

"I 'Like' Who I Am …I 'Love' Being Me!"

I like who I am, I love being me!
I am full of life, full of personality,
Easy-breezy, completely carefree.

I like being happy.
It's what I choose to be. And
Happy is the way it's gonna' be.
For **I like who I am,**

I love being me!

(Say it one more time)
"I Like Who I Am. …I Love Being Me!"

Animals in the '*Wild*'

Animals in the wild run totally free, away from city life, away from you and me.

They say I should wear something else besides my black and white. But, I can't help it. I really love my stripes!
I'm dressed for every occasion, for black and white is always in.
And if you say you saw me, they'll wonder '*Where have you been?*'
Who am I? "I am a <u>zebra</u>," and I like who I am, I love being me!
I live in the grasslands of Africa with very few trees.
I eat plain grass and herbs, shrubs, twigs and leaves.

I move a little slow because I think before I go.
They say I am consistent, but, it's the only way I know.
It takes me longer to go from point "A" to point "B,"
Because I have a heavy trunk. I carry a lot of weight-in-memory.
Who am I? "I'm an elephant," and I like who I am, I love being me!
I live in the rain forests of Asia, Africa, and the deserts of Mali.
In the savannas and grasslands I eat large amounts of herbal roots, fruit, and twigs, because I'm a bigger fellow.
I spend eighty percent of my day grazing on food from the meadow.

They say I'm quite inquisitive, but I just have a great view.
I can see everything above, below, and all around you.
You might see me on a safari, or you might find me at the zoo.
You'll recognize me right away 'cause I'll tower over you.
Who am I? "I'm a **giraffe**," and I like who I am, I love being me!
Like the zebra and the elephant I come from the same place.
I eat Acacia tree leaves, flowers, vines, and fruit;
For I can reach a much higher space.

They say I'm a little heavy, and that I should eat less junk.
They don't realize it, but I consider myself a hunk!
For the more of me there is, the more of me you'll see.
And one day you may agree that I'm as fine as I can be.
Please tell me, "Who am I?"

"I am a **hip-po-pot-a-mus**, and I like who I am, **I 'love' being me!**"
In the coolness of day, I eat water plants, for without sweat glands
I must adjust. At night, I eat fruit, grass, and other vegetation.
There are only a few of my species left in the nation.

Animals Closer to Home

{Here are some animals you might see almost any day.
Some are friend to man. Some just love to play.}

Most of my movements go unnoticed 'til I focus on a person or two.
But-t-t, I have more than one purpose.
Cheese and milk are my produce.
They say I'm amazing, because I am versatile and tough.
I eat grass, plants, tree leaves, herbs and stuff.
Who am I? "I am a <u>goat</u>," I like who I am, and I am loving me!
I'm the male, a "buck." The female is a "doe."
Please let your parents know, our baby is called a "kid." ☺
My skin is soft and furry-like, for
The finest cashmere and mohair come from me. That's right!

I bump and bounce, and jump from here to there. It's a habit.
It's what I do. And I'll go almost anywhere for my favorite food.
Who am I? "I am a <u>**rabbit**</u>," I like who I am, and I love being me!
Rabbits live in groups, mostly underground.
North America is where most of us are found.
We're in forests and wetlands, meadows green, and deserts too;
Eating alfalfa hay, and carrot roots is what we do.

Friend to Man

I'll stay by your side through thick and thin.
I'll be there to protect you. I'll let no one in.
That's why they call me man's best friend.

On this page of pet **dogs** you'll find a terrier, and a cocker spaniel;
A poodle, and a Rottweiler too. But, one of us gets haircuts.
Can you guess who? (See the hint below.)

Hint: If you're a special pet, good grooming is what you get.
But, you *ain't seen nothin'* yet,
until you've seen me with a fresh cut!
Who am I? "I'm a **poodle**," and I like who I am, I love being me!

Splendor of Color

*(Our feathery friends come in a splendor of color.
They fly in groups. They flock together.)*

As a baby I look like a chicken, but have the beak of a hawk.
But, as I grow up, you should stay out of my way,
Because I might give you a squawk.
And when I'm hungry I am as fierce as a hawk.
Who am I? "I am the **raptor bird**," and I love being me!

I have feathers. I have wings. Early each morning I chirp and sing.
I use my wings to help me fly, to make daily trips across the sky.
Just as the sun begins to set, I go to my nest to rest,
Then rise early in the morning to sing a melody.
Sometimes groups of us flock together.
There are many varieties of me. We're **cardinals**-both male and
Female, **robins**, **blue-jays**, a Momma and baby **canary**.
Who am I? "I am one of many **birds**," and I love being me!

(<u>Note from the author</u>: I love beautiful birds. Every time I see a **"cardinal,"** it makes me very, very happy. Yesterday, I saw five of them together in my back yard. There were a mommy {<u>female</u>}, daddy and 3 boy birds {<u>male</u>}. They visited for quite a while. Nov. 16th)☺

They tell me I talk too much, though I'm very polite.
I simply repeat what I hear, wrong or right!
I'm very colorful and bright.
You might think I'm a sight to see. People often try to imitate me.
I come in many colors, in many varieties.
They say I'm beautiful, and I agree.

Who am I? (You guessed it!) "I'm a **parakeet**."
I live in the tropics of Australia.
I feast on fruits, veggies, nuts and seeds.

My beauty is rare. It makes people stop and stare.
When I spread my feathers, nothing compares.

Who am I? "I am a peacock," as pretty as can be!
I eat insects and plants, and small creatures. You see,
The tropics and rain forest are home to me.

We Call It "Home"

We have the best life of all, for we live in the woods of the forest near the lake, by the pond; with all kinds of animals, deer, doe and fawn. And whether we crawl, or run, or casually roam, it's our special place. We call it "home."

And we play in these woods near the lake, by the tree. In the grassy terrain, far from city life, animals roam free. Whether we crawl, fly, or run, or casually roam, we just love this place we call "home."

It's the place where deer and antelope gather carefree. A special place too, for you and me; where both animals and people walk leisurely. Showing kindness to one another, both day and night, we all get along without fuss, or fight.

Yes. This is the place in the woods of the forest, where we casually roam. *This is the place we call "home!"*

~

How would you know that I'm pecking on your favorite tree,
Unless you get up early one morning, ...unless you hear me?
Who am I? "I am a **woodpecker**," and I like who I am, I love being me!
I eat the nectar of the flowers much like the bee.
When I fly, I hum a sweet melody.
Just to see me in action is such a thrill.
'Cause I'm in constant motion. I seldom stand still.
Who am I? "I am a **humming bird**," and I like who I am, I love being me!
Yes. We're "*happy!*" We're "*peaceful*," "*content* and *cared for.*"
God watches over each one of us, and so much more. ☺

Happy, Peaceful, Content and Carefree

We (too) can live life harmoniously,
Without any stress – completely carefree.

As human beings we understand,
That God had a special plan for man.

His great desire for us to live sin-free, came
When Jesus died on the cross at Calvary. (John 3:16)

By accepting His plan for our lives we become,
Through His grace and mercy, His chosen ones.
(1John 1:9; Romans 10:9-11)

Our body, mind and spirit begin to mend
When we accept His invitation to be our friend.

For we too, can live life harmoniously,
Without any stress – completely carefree.

<u>*Accepting His plan*</u>: (Please say this prayer out loud.)

"Dear Heavenly Father, Today I accept Jesus as my Savior, Lord and King, for I believe He died on the cross for me. Please forgive me for my sin. I believe, right now, I am born again. In Jesus' Name. Amen."

"Look at the birds of the air: they neither sow nor reap nor gather into barns, and yet your heavenly Father feeds them. Are you not of more value than they?"
(Matthew 6: 26ESV)

Prayer of Gratitude

Dear Heavenly Father,

I know that You care about the animals
But, You have a *special love* for me;
For You gave your only son, to hang on the cross,
And die at Calvary.

The confidence I have comes from spending time with You.
But, *prayer* is something animals can't do.
For You hear my prayers, and answer them too.

I'm so grateful that I can put my trust in You.
And 24/7, I can call *talk* to You.

Thank You for being my best friend.

Love,

_____
(Your name)

"Look at the birds of the air: they neither sow nor reap nor gather into barns, and yet your heavenly Father feeds them. Are you not of more value than they?"
(Matthew 6: 26ESV)

Animal Quiz:

Let's do some research. You will need a *dictionary, paper and pencil* to answer the questions below. Now, take your time and have fun. ☺

1. What is an animal? An animal is _____.
2. Define animal kingdom, plant kingdom, pet.
3. Is a mammal an animal? In which Kingdom do you belong?
4. Can you name at least five (5) animals not found in this book?
5. If you could add one animal to this book, which one would it be?
6. If you're not an animal, then you are a plant. T/F
7. Can you name 3 plants? _____, _____, _____.
8. Do you have a favorite animal? __Yes/__No. Which one?
9. Do you have a pet? __Y/__N. If yes, how many pets do you have?
10. List all of your pets. Describe each pet on your list.
11. Can you find a picture of a poodle with a fresh hair cut?
12. Name the wild animals in this book?
13. Can you name three other animals in the forest scene?
14. Which animal would you like to learn more about?_____
15. Look up information on the animal(s) you named in question #14. Tell us what you learned about this animal. (In two paragraphs)
16. *Enjoying God's beautiful creation.* Recently, I had a visit from five cardinal birds. *(Please see my author's note on that page.)* Looking at the colorful birds' illustration, describe the difference between the male and female cardinal bird.

Word definitions:

Adorable -- cute
Animal Kingdom -- scientific classification of animals
Attention -- aware; mindful
Awe (in awe) -- to be amazed; a state of pleasant surprise
Careless -- without a care; not concerned; free
Clueless -- doesn't know; doesn't seem understand
Cease (d) -- to stop; (stopped)
Confident -- very sure
Consistent (ly) -- continued; non-stop; did not stop
Determined -- will do it no matter what, will get it done
Favorite -- something you like more than anything else; like the most
Inquisitive -- curious; to be interested in
Personality (ies) -- character; your expression of "you"
Spellbound -- in deep thought about it; frozen in the moment
Sync -- altogether in rhythm
Unique -- unusual, different, not the normal way of doing things.

Lesson learned: God cares about everything. He doesn't want us to worry about anything. He takes care of the animals. And He certainly cares about you and me.

~

"Give all your worries to Him, because he cares for you." (1 Peter 5:7)
(If the animals can, you can too.) ☺

Want another **Leep4Joy Book**?
Go to: www.Leep4Joy.com

Leep4Joy Children's Books:

Happy To Be Me!
Happy To Be Me! Coloring Book

The Bully Met My Dad! ...and Became My Friend

Let's **"Love"** One Another
Let's **"Love"** One Another Coloring Book

It's Just a "Circumstance!"

It's About the Boys!

Fit-not-Fat!

I've Got a "Circumstance!" ...*But I'm Gonna Be Just Fine*

Adult/Teen Best Seller:
How To Overcome Every Obstacle and Land on Top
Bully Me?...Oh No!!! ...Suicide is not an Option

If you like our books please let us know: PatriceALee@gmail.com

Twitter: @ Leep4Joy

Facebook: Leep4Joy Books

Made in the USA
Middletown, DE
16 June 2022

67046486R00024